D0374583

LEARNING TO WRITE = LEARNING TO SEE!

Here is a unique new method of learning to
write that is as revolutionary as it is simple.
Based on the principle that all effective
writing depends primarily on accurate, insightful
observation, it teaches the student how to
see life with the perceptive eye of the great
photographer. Then, the student learns how to
express himself and what he has observed
in an entirely fresh and original way. Included
are examples of the work of such famous
photographers as Robert Capa, Edward Steichen,
Henri Cartier-Bresson, Philippe Halsman,
Marc Riboud, and Scholastic Magazine
Photography prize winners.

STOP, LOOK, AND WRITE!
THE CREATIVE WAY TO LEARN WRITING

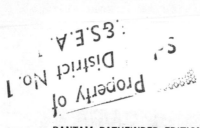

BANTAM PATHFINDER EDITIONS

Bantam Pathfinder Editions provide the best in
fiction and nonfiction in a wide variety of
subject areas. They include novels by classic
and contemporary writers; vivid, accurate
histories and biographies; authoritative works
in the sciences; collections of short
stories, plays and poetry.

Bantam Pathfinder Editions are carefully
selected and approved. They are durably bound,
printed on specially selected high-quality paper,
and presented in a new and handsome format.

THE AUTHORS:

HART DAY LEAVITT is a graduate of Yale University. Since 1937 he has
taught English at Phillips Academy, Andover. He is also editor of two books
for the Looking Glass Library.

DAVID A. SOHN is Instructor of English in Middlesex High School, Darien,
Connecticut, and Assistant Supervisor of Study Skills, The Study Skills
Office, Yale University. He is also the editor of TEN TOP STORIES, REVO-
LUTION IN TEACHING, and PROGRAMS, TEACHERS, AND MACHINES.

STOP, LOOK, AND WRITE!

EFFECTIVE WRITING THROUGH PICTURES

BY HART DAY LEAVITT
AND DAVID A. SOHN

BANTAM BOOKS

BANTAM PATHFINDER EDITIONS

NEW YORK / TORONTO / LONDON

RLI: VLM 6.0
IL 7.12

❦

STOP, LOOK, AND WRITE!
Bantam Pathfinder Edition published November 1964

Library of Congress Catalog Card Number: 64-7920

Contents

"What a strange way to learn to write: studying photographs!" It will surely seem strange if you never thought of the connection between language and seeing. Actually, the way you select words and organize them into whole compositions depends on the way you see human experience. If you literally do not see anything, you will of course have nothing to say.

The student who writes the following kind of prose —because he doesn't "see" anything better to write about —will always have a difficult time expressing himself, and he will be dull and bored:

> The main reason I like stamp collecting is that it is very interesting. I can always sit down and look over my collection; or if the latest stamp magazine is around I can look at that and read about the quotations of prices. If I find a stamp in the auction I want, I will look it up in a catalogue, find the price of if, and think what I should bid.

Such a student, if he never learns how to be more observant, very easily grows up into the sort of adult who on the witness stand, drives lawyers into straitjackets:

> "Mr. Acorn, will you tell the jury just what the man looked like?"
>
> "Well, it's hard to say . . . he was kind of . . . dark, I guess . . . had on a medium-colored suit . . . sort of . . . he wasn't really tall, but he wasn't short either . . . and he had on one of those what-you-call-it hats . . . had a funny way of speaking, too . . . sort of like . . . like . . . kind of . . . well. . . . You know what I mean. . . ."

On the other hand, anyone who has learned to observe, like the author of the following paragraph, is neither dull nor bored; for she has learned a superior way of seeing and writing:

Annabel and Midge came out of the tea room with the arrogant slow gait of the leisured, for their Saturday afternoon stretched ahead of them. They had lunched, as was their wont, on sugar, starches, oils and butter-fats. Usually they ate sandwiches of spongy new white bread greased with butter and mayonnaise; they ate thick wedges of cake lying wet beneath ice cream and whipped cream and melted chocolate gritty with nuts. As alternates, they ate patties, sweating beads of inferior oil, containing bits of bland meat bogged in pale stiffening sauce; they ate pastries, limber under rigid icing, filled with an indeterminate yellow sweet stuff, not still solid, not yet liquid, like salve that has been left in the sun.

—DOROTHY PARKER, "The Standard of Living"

What this book proposes to do is provide a method whereby both students and adults can learn something about the art and power of observation. You might call the method "A Beginners' Course in How to See." To "notice," to "perceive," to "see" in the best possible way, one needs to practice looking for such things as similarities, differences, emotions, gestures, colors, details, and conflicts. They are all part of the technique of the art of observation. Archibald MacLeish, the poet, has cited the goal: it is to learn to "see feelingly."

Every picture in this book has been chosen not only as a test of the ability to see merely literal things, but of the art and power to see the intangibles: character, feeling, images, ideas, innuendoes, and other ESP's. Difficult as they are to find, and to discuss, they could not be ignored in a book like this—a book on the power of observation—since they are really the main reason why anything is superior, good, and great, whether it is a movie, a book, a photograph, a bit of conversation, or a student "theme."

To speak strictly in educational terms for a moment, there has been much too much emphasis, both in teaching and in textbooks, on the learning of rules, especially picayune and mechanical ones—like the use of "like"—and not nearly enough stress on the kind of subject matter to which a student should apply the rules. Rules are not enough; a new approach is needed to help boys and girls find something lively and meaningful to write about. Through the study of photographs, this book aims to encourage young people to use their senses to discover things worth writing about, in precisely the same way that a good professional writer does.

To be very specific, one of the first lessons a professional newspaperman or a free-lance photographer learns is the importance of "human interest," or what is known among journalists as a "nose for news." What this book proposes is that students discover "human interest" by studying pictures taken by trained observers who know it when they see it.

Finally, this book is also about language. This is the crucial test: NOT just—Have you seen accurately and imaginatively?—BUT: Have you used language that faithfully and fully communicates to someone else?

Everything here aims at the expression of meaning in the most effective possible way, and this "meaning," this result of observation, must always include the PARTICULAR, the SPECIFIC, the DETAIL. One of the main reasons for using photographs here is that they emphasize particular details with staggering force, so that eventually anyone addicted to old abstractions like "good," "neat," "wonderful," "nice," and "queer" will see how futile they are, both as descriptions of the sharp reality in the pictures, and of the same sharp reality in human experience.

The original idea for this book was developed through nearly ten years of experiment with high-school students. In the process of preparing the presentation, it gradually became quite clear that the essential philosophy is applicable to anyone, whether in school or out, young or old, amateur or professional. Each one can learn the power of expression from the art of observation.

SECTION ONE:

The Image of Concentration

". . . that they which see not, might see . . ."
—ST. JOHN, 9:39

When you look at something, LOOK at it!

SECTION TWO:

First Try

How Much DO You See?

Study the following four pictures carefully. See HOW MUCH you can "see," and then write it all down, as if you had actually been watching the scene, and wanted to tell someone about it.

You may write this in any form—narrative, essay, or detailed description—but it will probably be more effective if you imagine yourself talking to someone who had not seen the old lady, or the gathering of students, or the political meeting, or the three young actresses waiting in the wings.

No elaborate instructions are given here about HOW to write, because the point is to concentrate on WHAT and HOW MUCH you have to say, as a result of observation.

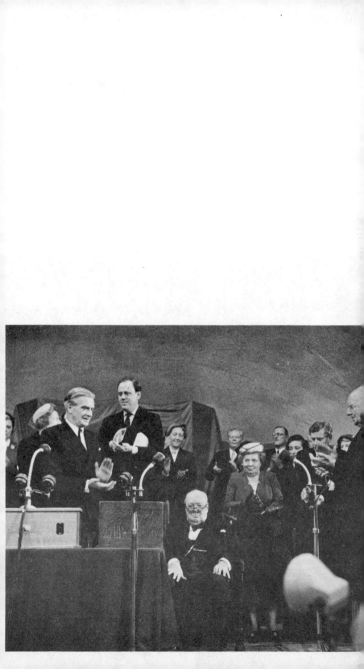

SECTION THREE:

The Power of Observation

Take a Second Look

All the pictures in this section are in a sense puzzle pictures, for there is something special about each one, which has to be discovered by sharp observation. For the student, the difficulty varies: in some cases, it is nearly impossible to tell what the photographer was trying to convey; whereas in others, perceptive study will reveal what is happening.

In the former instances, write your defense of an interpretation, with details from the picture to uphold what you believe. Where the "secret" can be determined, write about "it" in relation to the rest of the picture.

These pictures involve assignments in what is strictly called "the power of observation." You are to look for a meaning you do not know at first, but which may be there to be discovered, if you can "see" the right things and understand their relationships. Unlike later assignments, you are still not going to be held to a particular kind of writing: the emphasis here again is on pure subject matter—WHAT have you found to say?

Although the answer may be found in details, you should also listen to hunches, since the truth may be found in what you "feel."

In many cases, those who never find anything "special" in these pictures have to be told. Their reply is usually, "Why, I never even noticed that!" The whole philosophy of this book is that bad work, in school and out, is generally the result of the things you "didn't even notice."

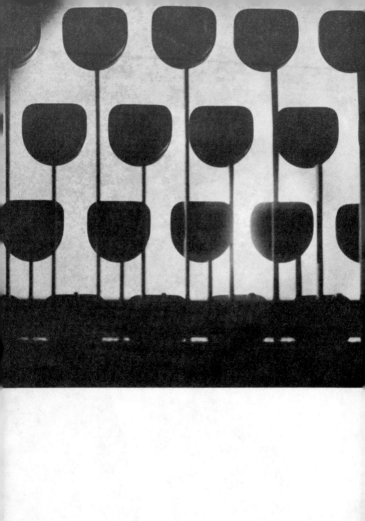

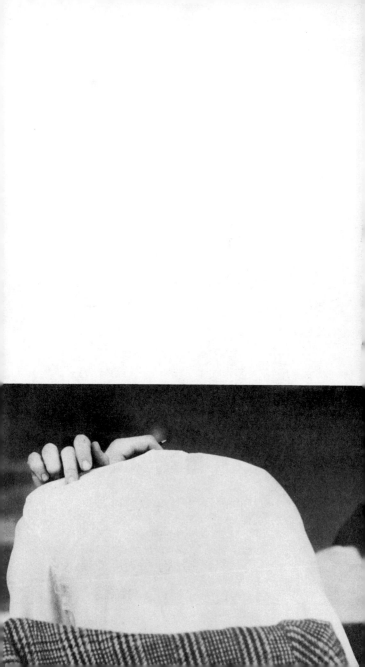

ON YOUR OWN

Can you remember a person, a situation, or a scene that at first you did not understand, but that later, through your own searching or someone's explanation, became clear?

Here is the basis for a good composition. On an experimental basis, try writing it in three parts:

1. A description of the subject matter, and a clear account of what puzzled you.
2. An explanation of the answer.
3. The effect of the discovery on you.

Or, you might write an explanation of why you did not or could not see the answer in the beginning. What details did you miss? What relationships did you fail to notice? What ideas occurred to you that were wrong?

SECTION FOUR:

The Art of Inventing Titles

. . . in a Few Words

A good title is brief and striking; it sums up directly, or by suggestion, the most important idea or feeling or action in a picture, just as it does for a painting, a motion picture, or a book.

As you study the following photographs, write single words as they occur to you. Then pick the most accurate and appropriate one as a title.

Next, try the same exercise with phrases of four or five words.

If nothing appears which seems satisfactory, try writing very short sentences that sum up the essence of the picture. This may be done directly: "The photographer was trying to communicate . . ."; or indirectly: "The doctor looked as if he wondered whether it was worth continuing." From such sentences you may find a suitable title.

One rather special way of finding a title is to sum up in very abstract words what you think the picture, even though it is very specific, suggests about general human experience. This is the hardest to do well, and the easiest to do badly; therefore it is good practice. Are any of the following effective?

Endless Infinity	The Way Things Are
In a Trance	"To Be or Not to Be"

When you compare your own efforts with others, ask:

Which words are the most precise?
Which title makes you say: "There . . . that's got it."
Which shows the most inaccurate observation?
Which is too plain and obvious?
Which one makes you see something you missed at first?

SECTION FIVE:

The Art of Comparison

Likenesses Are the Common Denominator

A small mind sees only differences,
a great mind: similarities.

Here, the specific theme is likeness, but the general idea is still the same: students write badly because they see and think badly.

To cure the patient, many educators attack the symptoms instead of the cause. They red-pencil the punctuation and skip the mind that made the punctuation—a mind that has to be trained to take in more than one thing at a time.

The sooner students begin to notice similarities, the sooner their writing will become more interesting, just as "She was on the beach in her baiting suit" is a more interesting sentence than "She wore a good-looking bathing suit." Furthermore, as students see what things are like, they will begin to have more to say; and this is a vital matter, for much of their difficulty in college is not being able to write as much as teachers demand.

Also, developing the habit of looking for likeness may produce unusual and significant ideas, especially when the first things noticed are the differences. These are obvious, as in the first two pictures. Go beyond the superficial differences, behind them, and through them . . . and search for the kinds of similarity that do not appear at first glance.

Many of the pictures here have been selected in pairs, with common denominators, and these should be observed before any writing is done. Compare all things, tangible and intangible: motion, dress, features, forms, and relationships. Then write out complete comparisons focusing on a single idea that shows the two pictures as variations on a similar theme.

Do not wander aimlessly back and forth between the photographs; organize your thoughts and observations, so that you can see them as connected strings of material.

Before you write anything about the first two pictures, study the following two compositions. Analyze them from the point of view of these questions: What is the similarity described? Is it interesting, dramatic, intelligent? How well is it developed, by details and by explanation? Which essay is better, and why?

The Cool Thing to Do

Why do girls go frantic at the sight of a singing star? Why do they dress wildly and wear signs proclaiming their admiration for him? Why do they shriek with joy, pressing forward to talk with him, touch him, or get his autograph? It is most likely that their only reason for acting like this is that they wish to be popular with their other teenage friends. They think that other girls will like them because they have met Tommy Sands, or another singer. For the same reason, they feel boys will think they are sharp and ask for dates.

For much the same reasons, the Princeton students were probably compelled to go to the football game. They must comply with the collegiate style of dress—trench coat and sports-car hat. Like the girls, they are at the game because it is "the" thing to do. If they had not come they would be called grinds or finks, and called down for lack of spirit. These are just small examples of the way our society forces people unwillingly into doing what is "the cool thing to do."

Realization

The picture of the teenage girls watching their singing idol appear and the picture of the spectators at the football game are both pictures of people about to have a thrilling experience. The girls have just seen their singing idol appear, they are surging toward him trying to get near him and get his autograph. The spectators at the football game have just seen a back pop clear of the line and break into the secondary. They are just getting to their feet ready to mightily cheer the brilliant run.

One important similarity between these pictures is that both were taken the split second the event occurred. The back was just breaking away and the star had just appeared when the photographer clicked the camera. Both the spectators and the girls had waited expectantly for a long time for this moment. They are oblivious to everything around them; they are devoting their complete concentration to one man. Their eyes best express their attitude of hope, wonder, and amazement. They are opened wide to absorb the whole scene, and imprint it, like a stamp, on their minds. This intense concentration is due to the realization that this was what they were waiting to see. The excitement floods over them like a wave and this excitement is what binds the two crowds together.

ON YOUR OWN

1. Write a description of two things that are clearly similar. "Things" may mean objects, buildings, actions, people, scenery—anything where the resemblance is striking.
2. Find a similarity between two things that few people would ever think of comparing. Write a description and explanation so that, despite obvious differences, the reader is impressed not only by the likeness, but by its importance.
3. Explain the most interesting similarity you have ever heard about, or read about.
4. Think of a commonly accepted similarity which you consider false. Explain why it is unconvincing, or superficial.
5. Describe the fundamental similarity between two good friends; or—and this would be a real test—between a good friend and an enemy.
6. Describe the similarity between a child and an adult.

SECTION SIX:

Contrast

"THAT's what makes the big difference!"

The most difficult part of this assignment is choosing important contrasts. It is easy to write about differences that are obvious and silly; but to describe those that "really mean something"—that is another matter.

The first point to remember is that it does not mean much to discuss differences that do not begin in similarities. In the first picture, for example, it is obvious that the subjects, the shapes, and the complexions are different.

But it is more significant to notice how the three figures do the same thing differently. Observe the expressions on the three faces, the suggestions of motion, and the spirit of the two girls as against the chimp. These contrasts would produce a composition of real interest, and if done well, of genuine entertainment.

Or, in the case of the next two pictures, it is easy to see that the two dogs present an almost entirely different appearance. This, however, is not so important or striking as the reasons why these differences exist. Even more important as a subject for writing would be a discussion of certain similarities as background for contrasts.

Following the pictures of the setter and the greyhound are two examples of how students developed contrasts, one weak, the other strong. Before writing your own, analyze the reasons why one is better, especially in the choice of material.

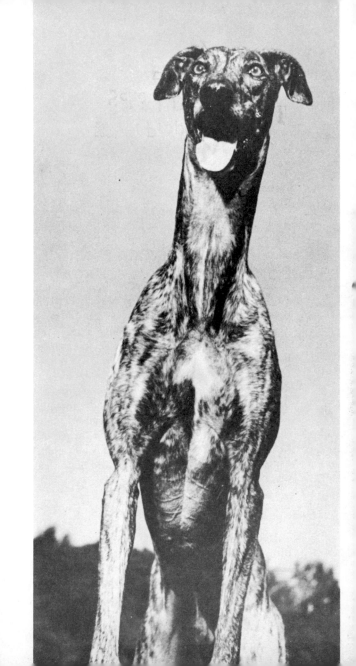

John and Fido

John was always an ambitious dog. He would work hard for his food by barking, digging holes in the yard, and playing with the children. When his master took pictures of John he would sit up and look as if he was ready to snap up a dog biscuit.

John's housemate on the other hand was more of a quiet dog. Fido would spend his days sleeping or wandering about the house. Frequently he would sleep in a chair with his shoulder pressed against the arm. Fido enjoyed life, for he knew he didn't have to work for his food.

John's and Fido's master was very fond of his dogs. He took their pictures many times and showed them to his friends. Most everybody thought that Fido was much older than John, because Fido looked so quiet and without ambition. But it turned out that Fido was younger than John; for when John died Fido lived another seven years before he too gave up the ghost.

Dogs and People

Dogs can resemble people in many ways. The pictures of the greyhound and the setter typify this resemblance.

The greyhound is the lean, athletic type of dog, always on the go. If he were human he would have a deep sun-tan from playing a great deal of tennis without his shirt. His leanness does not stem from the fact that he does not eat a great deal; quite to the contrary he eats all he can get, but still stays thin because he is always so active. He is quite healthy, and never refuses a game or challenge. He is so eager for exercise that when there is no one around to compete with he either competes against himself or goes out looking for a challenge. He is adept at every type of skill requiring great coordination or speed: scuba diving, surfing, skiing, tennis, or balancing on a bongo board, and he never gets enough of any of these activities. The look on his face best typifies his attitude: he is eager, so eager his tongue hangs out in anticipation of new adventures.

The setter, the greyhound's critic, is of a somewhat different nature. He is the more dignified and demure of the two. He frowns with disfavor on his energetic colleague. If he were human he would wear tweed, smoke a pipe, have impeccable manners, and engage in important philosophical discussions that would not interest Greyhound in the least. When Greyhound goes scuba diving, Mr. Setter stays home and reads about the state of the world. When Greyhound is playing tennis, Mr. Setter is going to the opera. When Greyhound is balancing on a bongo board, Mr. Setter is in the art gallery. He is concerned with life and the world situation, and was greatly disappointed that he was not chosen to be put up in Space (though he did step forward to serve his country, he was rejected for physical reasons; Greyhound got the job because of his excellent physical condition). He is indignant at times that Greyhound does not take life a bit more seriously but he forgives Greyhound's foolish ways. Greyhound, with much more insight than you would expect, also forgives his.

ON YOUR OWN

What is the most striking difference you ever noticed between two people, two places, two houses, two kinds of clothing, two ways of doing the same thing?

Explain the essential nature of this difference by relating to a point of similarity.

Conclude the composition by explaining why this difference is important.

Also, try these exercises:

1. Contrast a popular and an unpopular student.
2. Contrast your mother and father.
3. Contrast two brothers, or sisters, or cousins.
4. Contrast an athlete and a nonathlete, or an athlete who is only an athlete and one who is also a good student.

SECTION SEVEN:

Word-Pictures

"What a wonderful thing is metaphor!"
—CHRISTOPHER FRY

There is another version of thinking by comparison: seeing in simile and metaphor.

Most people look at one thing, and see it as just that one thing: they do not instinctively notice resemblances. As they watch an athlete, or a snowstorm, or a girl's face, or a sunset, they are not reminded of anything else. Or, if they are, the comparison rarely appears in their writing or their conversation.

Such "double vision" is usually the result of long training in the use of the eye and the mind, and the other senses. It does not come quickly or nonchalantly, except in genius.

This section focuses on the ability to see what things "are like," and to express that likeness in simile and metaphor. Emphasis, also, will be placed on appropriate comparison. The word "appropriate" is important, for students, when asked to find similarities, generally make bizarre comparisons; and they are not usually conscious of their grotesque imagos.

Try to perceive the spirit of your analogies, so that there is no wild conflict between what you see and what you are reminded of. A superficially clever, but very bad metaphor will illustrate this clash of feeling:

The leaves were lipsticked with autumn.

There may be some similarity of color here, but everything else is wrong, especially the clanking sound of "lipsticked." Nature is honest; lipstick is commercial —nature is natural; lipstick is artificial. In this instance, nature is not funny, but the comparison is almost a joke.

On page 31 you studied the picture of a country doctor, and then tried to compose a title. The same picture will be used here, as the subject of metaphor. First consider the following attempts. Which are accurate? Which inappropriate? Which silly, or clumsy?

He looks like a cop who has seen his first hit-and-run fatality.

A great despair clutches his spirit.

Reality has finally caught up with him.

His eyes are looking into the darkened area of destiny.

. . . a cigarette and a cup of coffee held by hands of mercy.

He's a boxer resting before getting back into the next fight.

The life of the patient, who has just undergone the operation, flutters like a curtain in the wind.

Time falls like the ashes of the cigarette, so slowly.

His tiredness is etched on his face.

If he doesn't watch out, he'll have ashes in his coffee.

His steady hands grip the cigarette and coffee unconsciously in the curtain of fatigue.

His hands held the saucer and cigarette as if they were surgical instruments.

The coffee had become tepid as old dishwater while cigarette ashes formed stagnant clots in the black puddle.

The following student metaphors will give you a genuine test of your imagination, for they are to be associated with a peculiar picture. Physical similarity is less important than imaginative, or spiritual, because the point of the picture is not what was photographed, but what is suggested by what was photographed.

Study these analogies, and then compare them with the picture on the following page.

1. It is a dead face.
2. This picture does not portray any feeling except conformity to a mold.
3. The heavy makeup and glassy stare of his eyes . . .
4. This is a picture of martyrdom.
5. It is a giant paradox: part of the bust is human, part is made of clay.
6. It has an indignant and haughty expression, like a goddess frowning down on the weaknesses of mankind.
7. The photographer was probably very cynical about mankind, and she was trying to bring out the bleakness of human existence.
8. A skin of white marble . . . and the aimless stare of eyes in death.
9. This face reminds me of men I know back home from the woods in Vermont, whose weather-beaten, leathery countenances show no feeling, and only their eyes express the workings of their keen minds.
10. These are the icy stare, the hard nose, and the tightly shut mouth of a ruthless, daring emperor.
11. The makeup makes his face as rough as a poorly plastered wall.

A good metaphor will always be visually sharp, and mysteriously imaginative. It will, almost always, be something of a surprise, too. One of the best tests to apply is the statement: "Why, I never thought of that before." If you can say this, and at the same time be impressed with the appropriateness of the similarity, then the metaphor is good. Finally, a metaphor should suggest more than it actually states, unlike the directions on a medicine bottle.

Apply these standards to the following professional examples:

1. "His face was a muscle playground, ugly, square and active—rippling with little spasms that might have been taken for thought."—John Hersey.
2. ". . . the trees were as bright as a shower of broken glass."—Christopher Fry.
3. "A lie can travel around the world and back again while the truth is lacing up its boots."—Mark Twain.
4. "Along the platform the patient sheep huddled together in thick clusters, their obedient toes upon the white lines painted on the floor. There was a roaring in the bowels of the earth, and a train, like a lighted dragon, ran out of the cave, its voracious body swollen with heads and shoulders and uplifted arms."—A. P. Herbert.
5. "The slow smokeless burning of decay."—Robert Frost.
6. "The great enemy of clear language is insincerity. When there is a gap between one's real and one's declared aims, one turns as it were instinctively to long words and exhausted idioms, like a cuttlefish squirting out ink."—George Orwell.
7. "To stumble in the spotlight never did anybody any good, and if the man who falls happens to be nineteen years old he may get an ego bruise which will leave him permanently tender."—Heywood Broun.
8. "Trust thyself: every heart vibrates to that iron string."—Ralph Waldo Emerson.
9. "Conversation in the feminine language consists of language rapidly vibrating or oscillating between two persons."—Christopher Morley.
10. "Modern colleges keep books like ledgers in which the student is reduced to credits, merits, hours per week, and weeks per year. They can fill him out in five minutes as sixty percent Christian, forty-five percent normal, assiduity guaranteed up to fourteen hours a day—saturation point—and intelligence tested five times under pressure and never burst."—Stephen Leacock.

ON YOUR OWN

Over a period of several weeks, write a dozen or so sentences identifying things which you know are unfamiliar to your classmates: actions, buildings, accidents, clothes, noises, shapes, people, etc.

The word "identify" has been used here, instead of "describe," to focus your attention more sharply on the idea of conveying the essence of what you see: that is, the most important part of anything that tells what it really "is."

Also, this time, in contrast to writing directly, which is what you do most of the time, write each sentence with a metaphor that suggests what a thing is—its identification—by showing what it is like.

As another kind of assignment on this section, you might compare the quotations on the "Toward a More Picturesque Speech" page of the *Reader's Digest* with the metaphors on pages 66 and 67 of this book. Which are more accurate, appropriate, effective, colorful, exciting, suggestive?

SECTION EIGHT:

Emphasis

"Do you see what I see?"

One of the most difficult and important aspects of writing is emphasis, saying something so that it stands out—like a lighted match on a blacked-out stage. Student writing is often weak because the good ideas have been poorly, vaguely, or wrongly emphasized, so that they do not appear to be more important than others.

One main problem is that students fail to decide beforehand, on the basis of observation and thought, what should be stressed. If they do make a strong case, it is often a matter of luck.

Study the following pictures and decide what is the most vital thing to say about each one. Then write a page or so leading up to the point. Arrange your details so that they all contribute to the main point, and be careful what you place just before the final statement.

In the process of writing the whole composition, practice on individual sentences, arranging the material in them so that one idea stands out.

The word "arrange" here refers primarily to the position in the sentence. English is basically a language of position, so that it makes a great difference WHERE you put your biggest ideas, and HOW you arrange the ideas around them.

As a general rule for all writing—sentence, paragraph, and whole composition—the end is the position of greatest importance, and the beginning the next. Finally, to emphasize a rule by breaking it, the weakest contributing ideas should go in the middle.

Study the placement of ideas and images in the following composition written about the picture on page 75.

The Sand

Billions of them are heaped up in great, white, dry mounds. They are jammed together, successively more compressed by others like them, until at the bottom of the mound the pressures exerted by each can only be measured in thousands of pounds per square inch. Still they are not crushed. Each particle of sand remains whole and intact, as if it were indivisible.

Those near the surface are whipped into space by pretentious blasts of wind and are carried for miles, constantly colliding with one another at frenzied velocities. They rebound erratically, crashing through the sea of mayhem that surrounds them, which is themselves. But they are not broken.

Finally they come to rest again heaped one upon another. They are intimate, especially those deeply buried, but they don't recognize one another. For they are all the same, and always have been, and always will be.

A plane falls, a thirsty man crawls, a wind blows, and they are in the air. They bury the plane and stifle the man, but they are not moved except by the merciless currents that jostle them aloft. The plane and the man are gone, and only a few of them know to where. But they will never tell, for they are like the others. They will continue to mutely shift, slide, and collide as they always have and always will.

ON YOUR OWN

Out of your memory, select a scene in which a great
many things happen at the same time:

1. The minutes right after a great athletic victory.
2. The results of an unpopular announcement before a crowd.
3. Confusion at home when several children all
   want the same thing at once.
4. The first few minutes after any kind of accident.
5. A large fight.

Write an account of this happening in which, though you
mention many things, you place them and express them
so that they all appear less important than one outstand-
ing part of the whole situation.

SECTION NINE:

Point of View

"Where were you?"

Students often hear their work criticized for lack of coherence, poor organization, and weak unity.

Though these are all good critical terms, the expression "point of view" will be used here, since it emphasizes the problem more acutely.

Look at one of your compositions as a purely physical matter: "Where was I standing in relation to what I saw?" This is one meaning of "point of view." Then, study your work with a different question: "What difference did the fact that I am a particular kind of person make in what I said?" These two queries are the foundation of control over point of view, since the organization, or the form, of a piece of writing is governed by the relationship between writer and subject matter.

For each picture, imagine you are a particular person observing the scene from a particular place, and that you have definite ideas about the time, the atmosphere, the people, and the conflicts. Then write these observations from the point of view of the character you imagine yourself to be.

For the first one, for example, which was taken at a ceremonial parade in Vienna, imagine you are (1) in the parade looking at the audience, (2) the officer with the sneer, (3) a policeman watching for trouble, (4) a spy from a rival government, (5) or an American tourist looking through a zoom lens.

Judge your writing by asking whether your words are those your imagined character would be likely to use, and whether expressions in one part of the composition contradict feelings, ideas, and attitudes expressed in another.

Here are two different attempts by the same student to write from a specific point of view about the first picture. Is one any more controlled than the other? Why?

"Twenty Years After"

I remember the day of the big parade. Thousands of people turned out to view a military show of might put on by the People's Republic. As military police, our job was to retain the crowd. We stood, arms linked, with a line of young schoolchildren in front of us. The youngsters were amazed and happy during the parade. Yet the little boy in front of me never smiled. His countenance displayed a frown. It was almost as if he knew, as I knew, that this parade marked the end of the Austria we had known. There was no more German People's Republic, no more war triumphs, no life without the party. Communism was our new way of life. The old ways and existence were over. This was to be our future.

As I look back, I remember a big parade when I was ten. The military strength exhibited then impressed me tremendously. All the other children my age were giggling with excitement and wonder. If I remember correctly, I was quiet. I looked up into the scowling face of the man in uniform behind me. He was frowning. As I think back now, his face seemed to portray the feelings of the adults. Disillusioned, they were seeing the end of their old way of life. I was seeing the beginning of my new life. And yet, as children often do, I mimicked the man, wearing a frown as the tanks and marching men passed. How foolish I was then. The Party is the only way of life. The Republic is life. There is nothing old, only the new.

ON YOUR OWN

The next time you see anyone in a fight or an argument, stop and observe—with the idea, later, that you will retell what happened from the point of view of one of the people involved.

It will be good practice, while the battle is on, to decide which one you have the least sympathy for, and then watch him (or her) very closely. When you write try to put yourself in the position of the antagonist.

SECTION TEN:

Seeing an Idea

"Do you know what it all means?"

In every assignment so far presented, one of th
great problems of writing and thinking has been implied
the conflict between the abstract and the concrete, be
tween the general and the specific.

Many failures are primarily failures in this area
failures in coping with abstractions, failing to be SPE
CIFIC. Most of the time, students do not realize tha
they are dealing with abstractions, and therefore have n
idea why their writing is weak.

This section focuses sharply on this difficulty. Th
compositions are assigned on abstract ideas as suggeste
by the pictures; and the development of each paper mus
include references to the concrete realities actually photo
graphed.

What an idea is, really, is a collection—an abstrac
collection—of concrete details. Democracy, for example
is an idea, a general form of government, an abstrac
theory, which in operation is made up of thousands o
individual, specific actions. Without these actions, ther
is nothing but a theory, which looks very good in th
dictionary. Precisely the same thing is true of such ab
stractions as terror, love, thought, education, corruptions
and rhythm. These are words; and words are alway
abstractions. Try and catch one.

Study the following pictures and decide on one gen
eral idea, or thought, or feeling suggested by details i
the picture. One way of doing the composition is ver
direct: expressing the idea and then illustrating it, almos
as if you were trying to prove it. The other is indirect
describing selected details so precisely and suggestivel
that no reader can miss the idea, even though it is no
stated.

The composition across the page shows how on
student developed an idea about the first picture. Almos
every problem in student writing is illustrated here, from
punctuation to choice of material.

A Child Walking Through Ruins

A boy is out walking with a knapsack strapped to his back. He is thinking that he is an explorer; a discoverer; the first person ever to travel "these parts." This is a game played by children in every country, and though the surroundings change, the excitement never does. This boy is universal.

The thing that sets this one particular boy apart from all the rest, is his strange surroundings. He is walking down a large set of stairs leading toward a group of buildings which have been bombed and are nearly completely demolished. Only concrete shells of their original forms remain, some large piles of rubble, and great gaping holes in the buildings, which add to the hollow and empty feeling. Many wild clumps of bushes, lining the stairs, fail to add any feeling of life.

The only living thing in the picture is the small boy. He is a contrast to the rest of the picture. He is in surroundings which are old and dead. The boy is young and alive. The buildings are bleak and harsh. The boy is soft.

There is a more important contrast in this picture, though: it is the one between what came before the picture was taken, and what is to come after it. The buildings show what came before. That was a generation that produced nothing but the war which destroyed the buildings. The boy signifies hope for what is to come. He is young, and has a chance to produce something out of his life which is creative, rather than the destructive things his parents produced. The boy signifies the hope of all mankind in their children. All people want their children to grow up with a better chance to achieve more than they themselves had. This boy, living as he does in the midst of ruins and death, and acting the same way any child might, by "exploring" the ruins, symbolizes these desires of mankind.

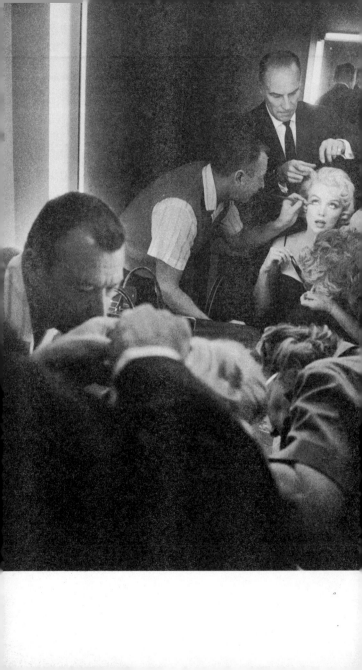

ON YOUR OWN

Take time off and observe a crowd or a group of people in action: at a meeting, a game, a restaurant, or a bull session . . . something like that.

Sit still, listen, and observe sounds, gestures, words, facial expressions, physical relationships, and attitudes between individuals: conflict, perhaps, or similarities.

Afterward, try to abstract from all these details a general meaning—an idea—about the way these people were behaving.

Write a fully developed paragraph explaining and describing your conclusion about what was going on. Use as many details as possible from the scene, and express the whole paragraph as if you were trying to communicate to someone who wasn't there.

Do the same thing by using the details, but never stating the general idea, or the abstraction, directly. Choose just the right things to make your reader feel the impression.

SECTION ELEVEN:

Conflict

No Contest? No Interest!

No short story, novel, essay, poem, or play would be successful without conflict. In fact, every work of literary art is based on opponents and opposition.

Only one student in a hundred, however, writes about conflict observed in actual life. Students prefer "nice" subjects, or subjects so abstract that it is easy to avoid tension, like "Friendship," "Education," or "My Philosophy."

Many people run away from conflict. Or perhaps they simply do not see conflict because they have never learned to look for it, except in athletic contests. Certainly they are surprised when conflict is required in what they write.

The pictures in this section are aimed at a search for conflict, so that eventually students will have, ready in mind, the kind of basic material that makes for good writing. Every one of these pictures reveals conflict. Some dramatize sharp physical opposition, some suggest it subtly; some reveal contrasts in line, idea, force, and shape; and some show a tight tension that does not appear in motion, but in a frozen moment of inner struggle.

1. Write one sentence that conveys a physical conflict dramatically, in any one picture.
2. Write one suggesting inner conflict.
3. Explain how one detail emphasizes a major conflict, or tension.

4. Write a full paragraph describing the atmosphere of tension captured in a picture.
5. Convey the conflicting forces through a metaphor. What is the conflict "like"?
6. Imagine the thoughts of one character involved in the struggle.

You have already done exercises involving problems in emphasis and point of view. In the following student composition, written about the situation pictured on page 101, these problems appear again as a young writer tries to develop the idea of conflict. Can you explain where this student becomes confused in emphasis, and also loses control of a coherent point of view?

Repentant

As I sat behind the table checking the refugee's identification I noticed how different this woman was from all the other people. She was dressed in German field grays. She said her boy friend had given them to her because clothes were so hard to get at the end of the war. Now her home had been destroyed, her friends and family killed, and she had nowhere to go.

Most of the other refugees had been recently released from German prison camps, and the guards were Free French with their typical berets. The war had so hardened most that they displayed no emotion toward the woman.

One buxom woman though displayed a violent hatred toward the German. I could understand the woman's hatred—she'd just been released from prison last week, and yesterday she'd learned that her whole family had been killed. I still felt sorry for the German woman who was receiving the butt of the hatred, for now she looked so repentant and sorry. I wondered how sorry the German woman would have looked if they had won the war.

ON YOUR OWN

1. Narrate a series of actions between two people who are obviously in conflict: boy–girl, child–parent, student–teacher, athlete–referee, performer–heckler. Don't use any dialogue; try to make the opponents move in relation to each other so that it is clear that they want different things, and that for some time these desires are opposed.
2. Do the same thing with dialogue.
3. Describe a series of actions between a man and a thing he cannot "push around."
4. Describe a very silly conflict between two people.
5. Narrate a difficult scene between one person and a group who want him to keep quiet.

SECTION TWELVE:

Character

To hold a mirror up to human nature

One of the most powerful forces in human existence is character. It is so strong that every writer throughout literary history has placed more emphasis on character than any other element. Students are made constantly aware of this fact as they study stories, novels, and plays. They are continually asked to consider the nature of this character, the thoughts of that one, the motives of another, and the way one individual is related to another.

In actual life, the importance of character and personality is so great that in the settling of human conflict, one of the first things considered is not just what a particular man or woman did, but how and why he did it. This involves the difficult task of figuring out what goes on in the mind, in the emotions, and in the instinct.

There are various ways of discovering such truth, but one of the most significant is the study of facial expressions, gestures, tones of voice, and movements of the body. These are the outward signs of thought and feeling, and though they may be misleading, they are so often right that they cannot be ignored. In the best sense of the word, no one can be called "educated" until he has learned, by reading these signs, to observe some of the great truths of character.

Such a study of character is justified by a fundamental moral principle: the understanding of other people. It is much like the process of analyzing characters in books, and this way of thinking can be transferred to actual life. Every good professional writer masters the skill before he writes anything worth reading.

The pictures in this section have been selected because they reveal character through expression, gesture, and action. Look carefully at the curve of a mouth, the glint of an eye, the lines of a face, the gesture of a hand, the posture of a whole body. What do all these details suggest about the individual? What traits would you expect to find in such people? What would you expect them to do in a conflict?

It may occur to you that these pictures show only one brief glimpse of character. This is true. You will realize only a limited understanding from these photographs. Yet this limited perception is important and realistic, for it is very like the limited perceptions you gain from actual observation.

In many of these pictures, the subject did not know he was being photographed, with the result that there is no doubt about the genuineness of the emotion. Even in the posed pictures, there is virtue in discovering what role the subject was trying to play, what "image" he was projecting.

When discussing friends, most of us can say nothing more than "He's a nice guy," or "What a dope!" or "Stupid!" We don't see enough to say "He's unselfish," or "She's shy," or "Don't be intolerant."

Close study of these pictures will yield many exercises. Here is a good place to do whole compositions: describe in unified form the meaning of relationships in a group, or the way one person is thinking. Another good exercise is hunting for single words that best capture the meaning of an expression. Or, try a metaphor to suggest what you see under the surface.

Finally, here is a chance to consider connotations. Although the dictionary may say the meaning is right, the sound of a word may be inappropriate, or its suggestions may conflict with something in the picture. One test is fairly reliable: if your language is greeted with a howl of laughter, you may be sure something is wrong, either with your vision, or your language. Here are a few attempts to analyze the character of the man on the following page. Try your own description. Then, characterize the people in the remaining pictures in this section.

1. I see a young Negro worker sitting in a darkened theater, excessively tired from a taxing day's work, meditating while awaiting the start of the evening performance.
2. I saw a curious Negro with baggy trousers sitting alone in a theater, his eyes focused on some very interesting sight.
3. In the front of a filthy deteriorated theater sat a tired Negro with well-used dusty clothing.
4. I see the utter desolation, loneliness, and solitude of the Negro race as portrayed by the lone black man sitting by himself in the tattered theater.
5. What I see is a desolate, poorly treated Negro sitting in his part of a segregated theater.
6. Sitting casually in a virtually empty theater is a Negro dressed in seedy clothes staring downward at nothing.
7. . . . one lonely Negro sitting slouched in one of the many seats, his large white eyes piercing the gloomy and eery dark.
8. I saw a perfect example of the sadness of the discrimination which has plagued our country.
9. He was sitting slouched in a chair looking beady-eyed at the movie screen.
10. . . . a look of complete hopelessness. . . .
11. . . . a very lonesome-looking Negro with his legs crossed, wearing sloppy old clothes, staring at a bug walking across the stage.
12. As I walked into the theater I saw, in the front row, a grubby decrepit hobo-type Negro with a somewhat guilty and preoccupied look on his face as though he was supposed to be working and his employer walked in.
13. . . . he looked as though he'd lost his last friend.
14. . . . a very dejected figure . . . sitting all alone in the front row, with no one else in the whole theater. . . .

ON YOUR OWN

There are several ways to tell about a person's character.

One is to come right out and say what he is, and then show how these traits appear in action.

Another is not to make any direct statements—"He was so selfish that he couldn't . . ."—but to describe individual reactions so clearly that the reader can't miss.

A third approach is to imagine what the person is thinking about, and then write out these thoughts so realistically that the reader will understand the person he is "observing."

Another way—a variation—is to narrate a dialogue, thus suggesting the nature of the person.

Choose one of these, or perhaps a combination, and write two or three pages about someone you know, trying to make the reader sense how this person feels, thinks, acts, and looks. Your objective is really to make your subject so clear that the reader can guess what he would do in another situation.

SECTION THIRTEEN:

Dialogue

"That sounds just like him"

For the following pictures, write a page or two of conversation, as you imagine it might have happened.

This is a logical result of the previous section, since conversation depends on character, as affected by situation.

Before writing, imagine who these people are, what they are probably thinking under the circumstances, what they are feeling, and what their voices would sound like. Seek also for a natural connection between their words and their actions.

Another approach is to imagine the nature of the conflict these people are involved in, and then develop dialogue that could be caused by the difficulty. Or, as a variation, in the case of the first picture, write dialogue that shows a contrast between the children and the scenery.

The most important thing is to choose language appropriate to the speaker, so that the reader "sees" what he may be thinking.

Finally, make the conversation lead up to a climax, to a positive conclusion from what has been said. The reader should finish with the feeling that the subject is over, at least for the time being, and that the next bit of talk will be about something else.

ON YOUR OWN

What is the most memorable conversation you ever heard?

Re-create it as if it were a scene from a play, and after each speech put in parenthesis a concise indication of how the words should be said, and how the speaker might act accordingly.

One obvious way to do this is to remember an argument. But, also, see if you can do a scene in which many ideas and feelings were suggested or hinted at, rather than laid on thick.

SECTION FOURTEEN:

A Good Story

What Happened?

To tell a story well demands much understanding and many techniques, and this section does not pretend to tell you all about how it is done: but it can start you practicing on several of the most important elements of narrative.

The first thing is to study all pictures in each series in order to make up your mind about the main idea you will emphasize. No one should ever begin a story without knowing the general purpose that holds all details together.

This "main idea" may be a thought, a conclusion, a comment, or a powerful emotion. Ideally, it should be suggested by all the details you use, so that when you come to the end, you won't have to spell it out directly in so many words, to the reader's face.

This result depends on selecting the right details from each picture, and rejecting others, no matter how attractive. Your job is to choose only those things that are important to the main reason you are telling the story.

When you come to the problem of putting your material in order, the main point to remember is that everything should be told in ascending order so that your tale rises up to a point of excitement or humor or revelation at the end. There should be a real contrast in strength between the various parts of your story, especially the beginning and ending.

In stories involving people, pick details to tell what the characters are thinking, even if their mouths are open. Here you will have to use your imagination, to figure out what their faces suggest that they may be thinking, as you did in the section on characterization.

Always, as you are planning and writing, make it clear that every sentence and paragraph adds something definite to the point of the narrative. You should be able to explain just what any given detail actually contributes. Test things by asking continually: "How does this relate to what I have just said?"

At some point in this exercise you should probably write out in so many words what the main idea or purpose is, for this will serve as a guide when you are choosing details; but most important, it will be the basis for what you say at the ending.

One thing you must NOT do is state a moral. It is a completely mistaken idea that a story must have a moral to be any good, and one has only to read a book of great stories to find how untrue this myth is. You can, of course, suggest a moral idea, or give a hint of some sort; but what you should really try to do is give the reader a surprise at the end. This may involve an idea about character, or a line or two of dialogue, or a specific detail of action, or some new thought about the whole sequence.

There are two good tests to apply to an ending, one for yourself, and one for the reader.

Imagine the reader looking up after the last sentence and asking, "Now what is that supposed to mean?" If you can say "It's just that that's the way things are," you have probably written a good ending.

Imagine, however, that the reader has the last word: "Why, I never even noticed that," or "I never thought of that before." If your last sentence makes him say this, you also have a good conclusion.

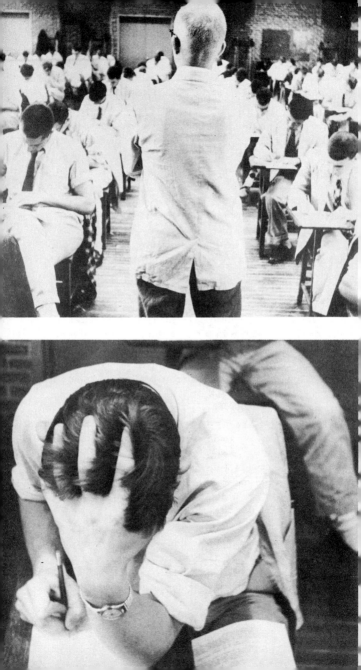

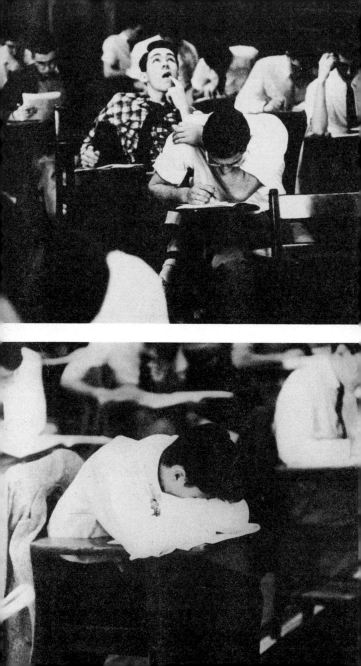

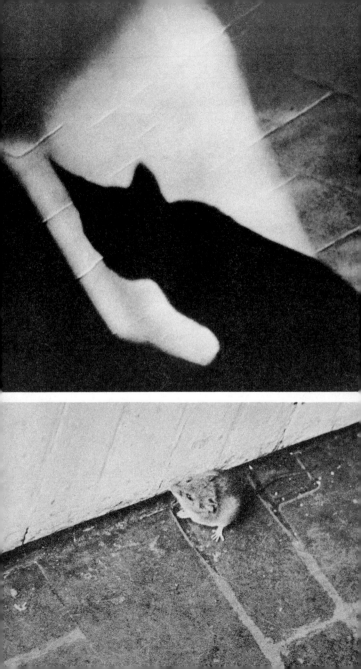

ON YOUR OWN

Pick a story out of your own experience . . . one that actually led up through a series of incidents to a climactic and meaningful conclusion.

Arrange the details in ascending order, and then write the story so photographically that the reader will be able to "see" what happened as if he had been there.

When you check through the first draft, ask yourself whether you have really SHOWN that the events happened, not simply SAID that they happened. The differences are revealed in the following paragraphs:

"From the way she acted, it was clear Jackie did not like the new boy in town."

"Jackie looked over his shoulder and waved frantically to another boy in a red convertible.

" 'Huh?' she said vaguely. . . . 'What was it you were saying?' "

SECTION FIFTEEN:

The Unexpected

The World is Full of Surprises

As you observe what people are doing and saying, and what is happening near you, look for surprises, for things you never noticed about things you have seen many times before. Out of such observation comes the best material for good writing. The purpose of this text is to point out not only that good thinking is the result of precise observation, but to dramatize the eventual fusion of the two in creative writing.

The trouble with student subjects is antiquity: the same old things are being written about in the same old ways, like stamp collecting, trips to the seashore, favorite hobbies, and that first date. You can, of course, write about the same old things in your own special way.

For practice, choose the most hackneyed subject you can think of, and write about it from a most unusual point of view. Or, write about a discovery made through unexpected observation.

The following pictures illustrate either extraordinary subject matter—the unexpected—or ordinary subject matter treated in an extraordinary way. Here, the observer looks, stops, and thinks. For each picture, write a full explanation of what the photographer has made you notice, particularly about what might have been a routine subject.

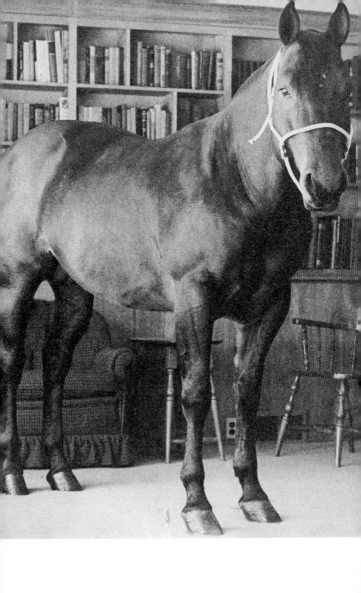

SECTION SIXTEEN:

Moving Word-Pictures

Suit the Word to the Action

The pictures in this section present a special problem: the use of language to suggest motion. This is difficult because of the contradiction that you will be trying to create a sense of motion with something that doesn't move—words. Literally, they stand still.

Their meanings, however, do not: and therefore, you must concentrate on finding words whose meanings are active. This is one reason why teachers object to verbs in the passive voice.

Even active verbs can sometimes be ineffective: verbs like "go," "use," "walk," "move," "act," and "take." Although they do convey some sense of movement, it is such a soft and general sense that no strong, lively, memorable impression springs up in the reader's mind. It's better to use words like "race," "poke," "mince," "slink," "show off," and "snatch" . . . as long as you don't use too many of them. The virtue of such diction is that it makes a sharp, clear picture of a specific movement that is not like a lot of others.

Or you can go further and use phrases and clauses, and other combinations of words which, when read together, convey a sense of motions happening together.

> She sat there, not eating much and keeping a sharp eye out for a vacant place on any plate and watching the jaws work, and as she sat there, her face seemed to smooth itself out and relax with an inner happiness the way the face of the chief engineer does when he goes down to the engine room at night and the big wheel is blurred out with its speed and the pistons plunge and return and the big steel throws are leaping in their perfect orbits like a ballet, and the whole place sings and glitters . . . and the ship is knocking off twenty-two knots on a glassy starlit sea.
> —ROBERT PENN WARREN, *All the King's Men*

Here is another passage, creating a different kind of motion.

> A stately squadron of snowy geese were riding in an adjoining pond, convoying whole fleets of ducks: regiments of turkeys were gobbling through the farmyard, and guinea fowls were fretting about it, like ill-tempered housewives, with their peevish discontented cry.

After studying the first picture, write phrases, or complete sentences, expressing the motion you see in the scene. Try to think in terms of the particular kind of motion your words suggest.

ON YOUR OWN

Write a sentence, or a phrase, describing each of the
following motions:

A car skidding.

A basketball going around the rim of the basket, and then
dropping outside (or inside).

A rock-'n'roll guitar player.

A jagged streak of lightning.

Cars on a freeway all going 70 m.p.h.

A car coming at you going too fast.

A girl flirting.

A football player avoiding a tackle.

A fishing rod bending as a fish runs.

An adult spanking a child.

A cop trying to hurry a slow driver.

Someone at a meeting trying to get attention.

The most characteristic gesture of an actor or actress.

The peculiar habit of a friend.

Someone smoking who doesn't know how.

Anybody showing off.

Smoke and flames.

A cat stalking a bird, or a squirrel.

Snow falling.

A water skier swinging out on an arc.

SECTION SEVENTEEN:

The Other Senses

There's More Than Meets the Eye

Most of this book is devoted to observation as a primary basis of good writing. But the other senses are vital, too, as almost all good writing reveals; for great authors have always worked hard to find the right words suggesting what they have felt, tasted, or heard.

Most young writers, however, are only dimly aware of sounds, textures, and odors, with the result that their compositions are flat and soft. In narrative especially, there is no feeling of reality because the characters are not surrounded by sensations.

Unhappily, when young writers do try to use the language of the senses, they often produce fake "mood pieces" filled with words like "gloomy," "eerie," "fantastic," and "hollow." This corn grows tall because the writer was simply shoveling up a pile of words; he was not using language to mean something he had actually sensed, or observed.

In this section, the pictures have been chosen because they show how the world can appeal to the senses. Look carefully at the smallest details, and imagine how they might feel, or taste, or smell. Find the most accurate and sensitive—and sensuous—words to communicate what is there to be observed and sensed.

In view of students' natural tendency to write purple prose, assignments for this section should be short: single words, phrases, or brief sentences. Metaphor should be tried also.

Do not wallow in adjectives, for the experience of the senses can be conveyed through nouns and verbs. It is especially good practice to work on nouns, for if the right one is found, then no adjective is needed.

How would you describe the combined
    taste of doughnuts, hamburger,
    and Coca-Cola?
Do it in one word
    ... or in a phrase
    ... or by a metaphor.
Describe it from the point of view
    of the soldiers, according
    to the expressions on their
    faces.

ON YOUR OWN

Go out and watch somebody eating a mess of sweets in a drugstore, or trying to study for an examination, or making preparations for a date, or reacting in an argument. Try to pick an action that involves more than one of the five senses.

Write about this little "slice of life" as if you were trying to imitate Dorothy Parker's picture of Annabel and Midge which was quoted on page 8. Make the reader smell the smells, hear the noises, feel the surfaces, observe the motions, and taste the food.

SECTION EIGHTEEN:

Imagination

To Make a World of Your Own

In Section Three, you studied scenes that were not clear. They either appeared to be something they weren't, or they resembled nothing you could recognize. With some of the logic of a detective, and the imagination of a poet, you discovered the truth.

For the pictures in this section, the purpose is not to discover the truth—in some cases it is pretty obvious—but to imagine things suggested by the pictures: images, ideas, visions, analogies, and, perhaps, something out of this world. The point is not, as in Section Three, to find out what the photographer actually "took," but to make up, to invent, to guess. What you communicate here is not what can be proven, but what you see in your mind's eye.

In other words, never mind "the facts."

If you get stuck, consider the following questions:

What might have caused this "thing"?
Have you ever seen anything like it?
What is it NOT?
What is the spirit of the picture?
What is the essential conflict or contrast?
How are the parts of the picture related?
Invent a scene of which this image could have been a part.
Is an abstract idea suggested?
Why do you think the photographer took the picture?
What is suggested by the shapes and forms?
Write a perfectly silly explanation.

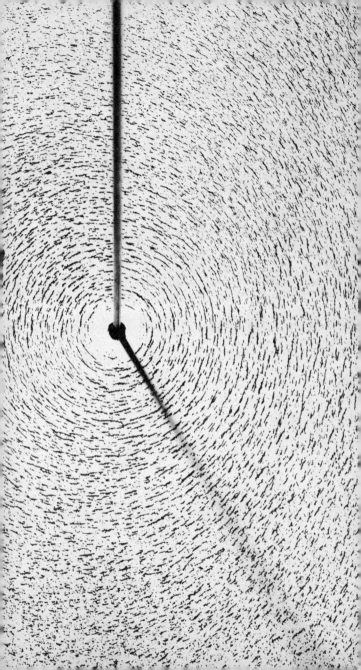

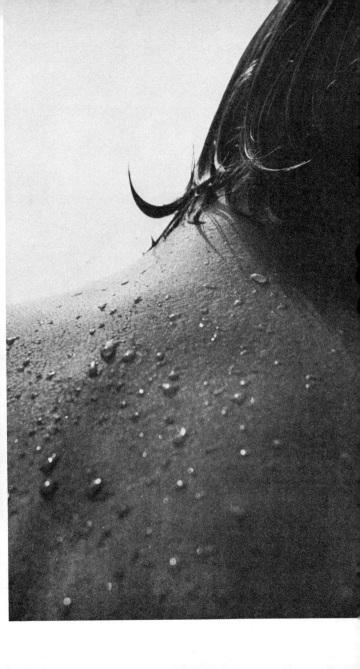

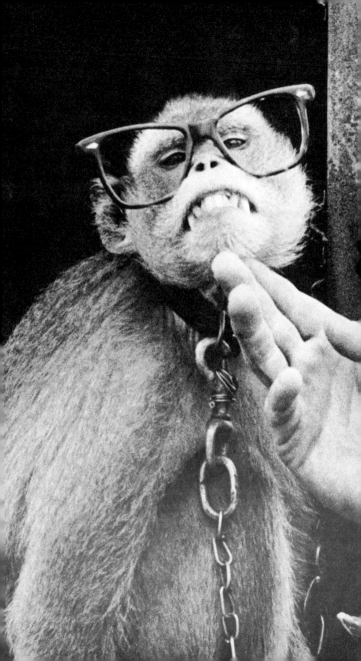

ON YOUR OWN

Think of the most puzzling, ambiguous, bewildering thing you've ever seen.

Describe it as clearly as you can from memory, and then sit back and try to imagine various explanations.

Choose the most likely one, work it out in detail, and write it down in full.

SECTION NINETEEN:

Corn

"He speaks nothing but golden banter."
—WALTER WINCHELL

One of the worst writing faults is triteness. It is also one of the hardest to erase.

When a student is told that his language is hackneyed, he is likely to explode: "How can I help it if I've never heard the expression before! How can I avoid clichés if I don't know they're clichés!" (One boy dramatized the whole difficulty by pronouncing the word "clytcha.")

Some textbooks do provide lists of clichés to memorize, but this is a mechanical method. It is far better to attack the problem from the point of view that no one will sharpen his language until he sharpens his vision, since accurate, emphatic diction results only from seeing the world in an accurate, emphatic way. Trite words come from trite thought; and trite thought is nothing but trite observation.

People who say "great," "nice," and "fabulous" do so because they have nothing in their minds but the vague pleasurableness suggested by such tired words. To describe character, for example, with words like "unselfish," "finicky," or "calculating" requires the ability to see these qualities with the eye and the mind. To see the weather as "murky" demands a different quality of eyesight from the kind that sees "lousy."

The function of this section is to dramatize trite thinking and observation so that students can see for themselves what they are doing. The point is to match stale language against a sharp image.

First, study the picture opposite, and then compare it with the "composition" on the following page. What's wrong?

Eerie

The night was dark as pitch as a lone, solitary figure wended its weary way through the pea-soup fog. The only light showing sort of seeped out from a queer-looking old street light next to a railroad crossing where the crossing guards stuck up in the air straight as a ramrod. I couldn't see too well behind them, but I got a hunch there might be something awfully spastic around. It was all kind of eerie. It gave me the shivers, sort of a creepy, crawly feeling. I expect the guy in the picture was soaked to the skin by the lousy fog, and he was probably trudging homeward to get right up next to a cozy little fire, and the cozy little woman, and pour himself some of that beer that made Milwaukee famous. He looks as if he were walking at a snail's pace, like he was kind of groping his way. Except for him, everything looks quiet as anything, and silent as the grave. This spooky atmosphere is highlighted by a funny light shining through a signal-like tower, fanning out flashlight-wise.

Now, write your own description.

To intensify the emptyheaded sound of clichés, a group of hackneyed expressions are listed below, in contrast with original images created by professional writers. The difference between them is a matter of invention.

1. He tried to snow the girl.

   "Marrow stood in front of her flexing his jokes."—John Hersey

2. That book is really something!

   "Reading that book will put your eyebrows on stilts."—Walter Winchell

3. He talks too much.

   "He's a man of a few thousand words."—Samuel Goldwyn.

4. The audience coughed so much you couldn't hear yourself think.

   "The audience strummed their catarrhs."—Alexander Woollcott

5. It was one of those real cool nights . . . you know what I mean?

   "The park is filled with night and fog,
      The veils are drawn about the world,
   The drowsy lights along the paths,
      Are dim and pearled."
         —Sara Teasdale

6. You jerk!

   "You dried neat's tongue, you bull's pizzle, you bolting hutch of beastliness. . . ."—Shakespeare

On the opposite page is a picture of one of the most frightening high-wire acts the world has ever seen. It was staged three thousand feet above the craggy rocks of the Zugspitze on the Austro-Bavarian frontier.

The ordinary tourist, if he saw this act, would probably come home and say, "You should have seen the spine-chilling thing we saw last summer. . . . Boy oh boy!"

There is no doubt about the chills going up one's spine on looking at this picture, but there is also no doubt that the word "spine-chilling" is pretty feeble beside the reality in the photograph. The trouble is not that clichés are wrong; it is that they are old and smooth, and pass through the ear and mind like warm wind. Also, they may cover so many meanings—like "exciting" or "dull"—that they do not convey the particular, individual, special meaning of what actually happened.

It is often said that a picture is worth a thousand words, and it would be dramatic if we always had pictures on hand to help us say what we want. But most of the time we are thrown back on words. The only way to learn to communicate expressively and quickly is to study what you see, and study it intently, until you know what the most important thing is, and what words most exactly describe it.

Make a list of all the clichés you can think of to describe this picture—and what this means is the actual reality in the picture—and then try to write a sentence that not only expresses your observation, but expresses it with originality.

Just for the fun of it, write a long corny description of the picture opposite, imitating the style of the composition written about the first picture in this section.

ON YOUR OWN

Study the following clichés in relation to the pictures indicated. Can you explain now why they sound so silly?

What is the most interesting incident you can remember? Write a page about it, using the worst clichés you can think of. Then do another page, trying to be as accurate and suggestive as you can. Try making up your own expressions, and using usual words in unusual combinations.

SECTION TWENTY

Humor

Life Can Be Funny

For each of the following pictures,

1. Write a one-word title.
2. ... a phrase.
3. ... the most suitable line of dialogue from one of the characters.
4. ... the most appropriate thought from the mind of one of the characters.
5. Find the most applicable quotation.

Explain an abstract idea suggested by the picture.

Write a brief character sketch of the kind of photographer who would take such a picture.

Explain why you think any of these pictures are obvious, or unexpected.

Suppose you heard someone say, "I don't understand why they print such stuff in magazines." Defend the picture.

Explain the most important comparison or contrast that makes the picture effective.

ON YOUR OWN

From memory, write a description of several scenes that are most similar to those in the preceding section, or most different.

Or, if you can't remember anything appropriate, make up a scene that would resemble one picture. You might approach this from the point of view: A Picture I Would Like to See.

One Final Exercise

Go back to the first four pictures (pages 17–20)—of the old English woman and her teakettle, of the crowd of students, of Churchill amid applause, and of the three young actresses—and write new compositions based on what you have discovered about the powers of observation.

Then, set these beside the first ones you wrote, and analyze fully what you did differently, both in seeing and writing.

On the basis of this experiment, study the following group of pictures—including the picture story of the little girl card player—and write the most fully developed compositions you can invent.

Consider this final test as both quantitative and qualitative: Did you notice any MORE things, and Did you notice different KINDS of things?

Then, compare these last efforts with some of the student writings that begin on page 204.

The Students Write

About the Pictures

The professional writer develops his art, like professionals in other fields, by studying the successes and failures of other writers, ancient and contemporary. In fact, most writers never write well at all until they know something of the history of literature.

Otherwise, like high-school students, they write in isolation, perpetrating and perpetuating the mistakes of others. In a sense, they are like many TV writers, palming off as new and good, stories discarded fifty years ago in the movies.

This principle of continuity should be observed in education. As young writers are learning diction, sentence structure, and choice of material, they ought to know what their predecessors did, and what their fellow students are doing now: good writing to see what is possible; bad, to avoid conventional errors.

It would be helpful, for example, both for teacher and student, if a boy in Massachusetts who says, "But I didn't know these were hackneyed words!" could be immediately shown compositions from Nevada, Mississippi, Florida, and New York, with the same clichés.

It would be helpful, too, for a teacher trying to convince his students to abandon stories about dope addicts, if he could demonstrate how bad a composition can be when the writer doesn't know what he is talking about.

These are two of the main reasons for concluding this book with a collection of students' work based on pictures throughout the text. There is the further point, moreover, that students may gain good ideas for compositions by studying the work of other students.

In the following short composition on the picture on page 17, a ninth-grade student reveals an unusual ability to observe detail with remarkable accuracy and completeness.

Fanny's Quaint Appearance

Fanny may be poor, but she is not forlorn as she prepares her tea. Though she is old and wrinkled, she stands straight and holds her head high. She may once have been beautiful with those deep-set eyes and arched eyebrows. Obviously she has few if any teeth and will probably eat something like crumpets with her tea, which she pours from a burned and blistered kettle into a modest little teapot. Her costume is unique, with its sweater covered by a figured apron top and a skirt which seems to be made of burlap, frugally patched. Since she is taking tea she has donned her best hat at an offset angle to add color and life to her costume. This rather interesting hat is the only expensive-looking thing in the room and leads you to wonder who gave it to her. Perhaps she picked it up for sixpence in a Thrift Shop. The torn wallpaper and old board ceiling, from which most of the plaster has fallen, are separated by a wide crack. This is the kind of house where termites like to work. On the wall hangs a curtain, which hides a modest window, a calendar, and a picture. The mantel is covered with letters and papers doubtless sent by her friends and children. The mantel drape is decorated with a design which may be needlework done by Fanny in an effort to relieve the drabness of the room. A metal hood partly covers the fireplace, in which we see some twigs. We do not need to feel sorry for Fanny, whose capable hands seem proof enough that she can take care of herself.

The following essay was written about the three women on page 54. Read it and then consider the question at the end.

"To Have and Have Not"

Many humans have a strange and unrelenting desire to obtain certain elements of life which do not belong to them. Many people daydream, placing themselves in famous men's shoes or just pretending that they are great athletes or millionaires. Rarely are we satisfied and thankful to have that which belongs to us and be who we are.

Perhaps this greedy desire stems from the competition in life. Some people might think that they are failures just because they don't have two cars. They are therefore inclined to wish that they had that second car—and a lot more besides.

Nothing can illustrate this point clearer than the picture of the two old, wealthy women walking in front of a poor pedestrian. One can see on the onlooker's face, an awed expression.

"How could anyone ever have a coat like dat. Gee, Whiz, dat's A-1. Look at dem lips and dat hair. "WOW!"

And for many days, even weeks, hence that onlooker will be walking in the same shoes, the same coat, her lips smeared in red, her eyes gleaming, and with the slight smile of wealth on her lips.

Is this interpretation justified?

One of the great arts of writing is invention, making up something that did not exist before. Here is what one student "made up" after studying the two pictures on pages 56–57.

War Lords

We were very confident, of course; the little hick planet was sure to be a pushover. After all, Earth was the most powerful planet in the galaxy; in fact, every one of our soldiers was really an army all by himself. With his flame thrower, space warper, gas bombs, bacteria culture, and small, fifty-megaton, tactical, fusion grenades, the average G.I. could take on a whole village of maybe more than three thousand people and completely wipe it out. Yes, we certainly had a right to be proud of our men: they were the best, bar none!

Well, the invasion, scheduled for the middle of summer, started off perfectly. We made a beachhead on the biggest continent—only the size of Greenland, believe it or not—and it wasn't long before the inhabitants were in full retreat—I guess they hadn't been used to fighting! You should have seen their men—amateurs! Why, they looked more like Sunday picnickers than soldiers: they were loaded down with all sorts of truck—shavers, pans, egg beaters, and the like. It was almost funny watching them die.

Pretty soon, though, even though the top brass were keeping things pretty well under cover, we got the word that something was going wrong. We didn't even need the word from upstairs—you could tell by just counting the men in the squads—plenty more than there should have been were gone. First we tried keeping better guard around the camp, figuring that maybe the enemy was kidnapping our men. It didn't do any good, mostly, I suppose, because it was during the battles that they disappeared—every night there'd be fewer and fewer fellows reporting back.

It took us a long time to figure out what was going on—I guess we were fooled into thinking that the enemy was completely helpless. What a bunch of sneaks—they had a secret weapon all along and didn't even let on: every time one of our men tumbled into their camps, they just sort of offered him food, told him to take his pack off and relax. Well, you can see easy enough what this kind of trick would do—when the guys shed that 250-pound pack, had a little coffee, and maybe even smiled for the first time in six years (we were kinda serious in those days), they went plumb off their rocker, got so shook up that they couldn't find their way back to our lines, and had to stay in those pleasure resorts the enemy calls their camps.

Funny thing, though, us, the most powerful world in the universe, we had to leave on account of all our troops disappearing—yes, sir, just about all of them got trapped. We ain't ever been able to take that world since, neither. We don't even dare go near 'em —the dirty hick amateurs!

The following dialogue was written about the political parade pictured on pages 72–73.

Wendell Willkie and John Versus Emma

"It's sort of exciting having the presidential nominee riding through our town. Don't you think so, Emma? He looks so distinguished riding in that handsome black car with a chauffeur and all."

"I'll tell you what I think, John. I think you need new glasses. That man's about as distinguished as a drunken salesman. Look at how his eyes bag out of his head! And look at that tie! There must be every color in the world swimming in that tie. Let me tell you, John; I wouldn't vote for that . . ."

"Oh, shut up, Emma. You know you're just trying to put on an act. You're as excited as anyone. Doesn't it kinda do something to you to see all those American flags. I'll bet there's four of 'em on every post in town.

"Hey! Look . . . he's wavin' to us, Emma. God! He's standing right up and waving to us. I'm going to vote for him, Emma. How about you?"

"I think it's disgraceful the way the people in this town act. Look at them, screaming, and hollering and behaving like a bunch of kids. I can't see but two jackets in the whole crowd."

"Oh, for goodness' sakes, Emma. It's ninety degrees. Look at all those black cars. I wonder what those big cardboard numbers are for: the ones on the windshields."

"Let's go back to the farm, John."

The following composition was written about the three Germans pictured on page 114. In addition to the usual problems—mechanics, diction, sentence structure, etc.—study the organization of the essay as a whole. From the point of view of placement of subjects, how has the student changed the emphasis from the picture?

War

In this photograph I see three men expressing their emotions of the war without ever speaking a word.

The boy seems new to the brutality of war and sits, silently staring into his cup. However, the signs of war are already present in the empty look in his eyes. I don't think he has grasped the reality of war, but he has probably had his first glimpse of the useless slaughter that surrounds him. He is probably wondering how he became engulfed in the nightmare of war.

The soldier without a shirt has probably seen many massacres. He has the look of a man who knows what it is to gore an enemy soldier for no other reason than that he is just "the enemy." He seems to be thinking of home and all the things that he may never see again. On his face are the outlines of many a day of fighting on a bloody battlefield and many a night in a rat-infested foxhole.

The third man is just staring. He has been through so much that his mind can no longer grasp reality. The endless days of seeing his old friends torn down by enemy fire have drained him of all emotion. All he sees now is the desolation that can be the only outcome of war.

On these three men's faces, I see what destruction war can do, not only to men's bodies, but also to their minds. These men will carry the memory of the horror of war with them long after they leave the battlefield.

Contrast the following compositions, one written as straight exposition, the other as "stream of consciousness." Picture on page 116.

The End of the Road

The carnival was closed now. The bright floodlights, the din of the crowds, the gaudy music, and the woody smell of the rides had all disappeared. To take their place was only the clank, thud, and shuffle as the brawny workmen hastily disassembled the mechanisms and the tents; the seats, the food, the sawdust—all were fading away. Several huge trucks had pulled up the ramp and were being loaded with what pieces of equipment the show itself owned. The drivers stayed in the cabs while the hired workmen assailed their duties. On the truck at the left, somewhat apart from the others, two men were engaged in loading a heavy steel horse from the merry-go-round. In the truck one of them, bare-chested, pulled at the top while his friend, sweating in a grease-stained jacket, pushed from the bottom. Their muscles bulged until their charge had been lifted into the truck; they had expended their energy for a moment. To the rear of them, another cart brought more material to be loaded. The men paused for a moment and surveyed the oncoming vehicle. The man at the bottom seemed angry. He was defiantly —yet expectantly—awaiting his future. The man on the truck took a different view. He was calm. He was a big man—and seemed not to care about his next job. He knew he had nothing to fear.

No Strike

Here they come back from the strike negotiations. Those guys are crazy! I've been working on the fair circuit for over five years and I know that they'll never get those benefits that they're asking for. New hydraulic lifts and better housing are just out of the question. Why don't those guys smarten up and realize the facts. Sam and I here, well, we know from experience that that strike stuff just gets you thrown off the lot. They don't realize that the boss is doing them a favor by giving them a job, because otherwise they'd be just ordinary unskilled, unemployed jerks. They don't even know how to put one of those merry-go-round things together. That's why Sam and I are doing it now. I can really laugh at those guys, because they don't even know what they're missing by striking. Yes, I have a good life and I don't complain. I've got money for cigarettes and all the drinks I want, and even some left over. I've got a future and I'm sure glad that I'm not mixed up in no strike!

In attempting to characterize the two roustabouts, both students have been inconsistent in language: at certain points, words suggest one kind of personality, but at other points, a contradictory kind.

The Model

From the very first moment that I saw her, a suspicion grew within me that maybe she really wasn't the detestable person she appeared to be. By everybody she was considered a cruel, thoughtless person, lacking any kindness; but, after I had seen her on very many occasions, I began slowly to discard this popular opinion. There was no doubt that the things she did to people were cruel, but after I became accustomed to her heartless actions, I studied her face and the emotions which others could not seem to perceive. I was surprised and almost delighted as I began to notice day after day an almost imperceptible glitter of compassion, shame, and misery. I saw only these, and to me her other self was only a mechanical impression, a false character.

This short character study, written about the model on page 112, raises the controversial question of meaning: Is that what the picture reveals? Even more important, however, is the other question: Has the writer developed his debatable idea thoroughly and persuasively?

Then, compare the following little essay about the two dogs on pages 50–51.

In nature one may find beauty in softness as well as harshness; for example, a common house dog is beautiful; his beauty lies in the softness of his eyes, his large, furry ears, and the touch of sadness at the edge of his mouth. The animal radiates a certain warmth . . . an inexpressible glow . . . as it curls up by the fire. Yet, isn't the sleek, stubbled-haired, muscular type of dog also beautiful? Though his coat of fur does not shine, and his ear are crooked, he still may be deemed a lovely creature; however, it is not because of his attractiveness, but rather his forcefulness and aggressiveness that he is elegant. His pulsating veins, the alert eyes, the hot, panting breath combine to form an image of power and speed . . . an image of beauty.

In the following monologue of the imagined thoughts of a soldier seeing the children on page 123, how clearly is the character of the "thinker" suggested by his words and what he notices? How accurate is his observation, and how convincing is his imagination? Is the composition "corny"?

Damn This War!

Boy, am I glad that's over! We finally chased the Germans out of this little Italian village, but not without a real battle. Most of the village has been completely leveled, and what buildings that are standing are just four walls and no roof, and many of the walls have big holes in them. Like that building over there. Hey, what's that sound coming out of that hole? Sounds like a bunch of kids having a great time. I think I'll check this out.

Well, how about that! It is a bunch of kids, playing in this rubble-filled alley. Even after all that shooting and killing and fear last night, they are playing this morning. Kids are amazing. Look at those two boys in the center. The one in the black skirt-like clothes must have been kidding the one on crutches, and the one in the white just has to get into the act. He's probably just showing off for his girl friend back in the audience. At least they all look like they are having fun, even the one on crutches.

That one little girl leaning against the wall on the right seems to be afraid of me or my gun. Maybe she thinks I'm going to kill her. It just shows you what war will do to a person. In peacetime, or at least before this war, seeing a gun probably wouldn't have bothered her. Now she knows that a gun isn't just a good way of getting food, or, for some people, of having fun, but a good way of killing people. I know just how she feels. The fear she has now when she sees my gun is the same fear I have before a battle begins—a fear of being killed. I can't wait until this war is over, and I suppose she can't either, so just one week will pass without knowing this fear. I suppose some people, like the rest of these kids, have gotten used to this fear, having experienced it so often. But not me, or that little girl. I like her.

I wonder what that bigger girl has in the basket she is holding. I hope it's food for these kids. There isn't much food around these days. The Germans took most of it, and left all these people to starve. We have given them what food we could, but that isn't too much. Maybe after we chase the Germans a little father north, they can do some planting. It's just about the right season. But what will these people do for food until the crops are ready for harvesting? I hope they have some put away someplace where the Germans didn't get at it. We sure can't support them until then. Hey! I wonder where the parents of the kids are at? If they are still alive, then these kids will be all right, but if they were killed . . .

Everything is so confused. Damn this war! If it wasn't for this war, these kids and their parents would be enjoying life with the rest of their families, I could be home with my family, there would be plenty of food for everybody, this fear would never have existed, and all this suffering, death, and wreckage would be happiness, life, with meaning, and a beautiful country with nice homes. Damn this war!

A Fable

(This fable is based on the picture of the cat and the mouse on page 148.)

Once upon a time there lived a cat named Sylvester. One day, as he was making daily patrol of the kitchen, he came upon a mouse named Ernest, who was caught in a trap.

"Help!" pleaded Ernest. "Please set me free."

"Why?" asked Sylvester.

"Don't you like mice?" queried Ernest.

"Sure I like mice," answered Sylvester, licking his

lips and rubbing his fat little belly with his furry paw.

"Well," replied Ernest, undismayed, "I like cats too, and I'd like to be your friend."

"But how do I know you're not a rat?" asked Sylvester.

"Why don't you smell me and find out?" suggested Ernest.

Now the truth was that Sylvester had lost his sense of smell after a spring cold two years before, but he was too ashamed to admit it. So, he sniffed a few times and said, "Well, I guess you're a mouse all right." Then he set him loose and the two became friends.

A few days later, as they were running and playing and singing "Three Blind Dogs," Sylvester complained that he was hungry.

"I know where there is some cheese," said Ernest. "Come on."

Sylvester followed Ernest to the kitchen door, where Ernest told him to stay and keep watch. Ernest went inside to find the cheese.

"Lend me your tail," called Ernest. "I need something to hold on to."

"All right," answered Sylvester, and he stuck out his tail as far as he could.

Suddenly something snapped on Sylvester's tail.

"OW!" he screamed. And on turning around, he found that his tail was caught in a mouse trap.

"My tail is caught! he exclaimed.

"I know," said Ernest, "but I have the cheese." And off he ran as fast as he could to the safety of his hole.

"Why, you weren't a mouse after all," called Sylvester. "You were a rat."

MORAL: A pleading Ernest is a rat in earnest. Or: if you don't know a rat when you smell one, don't stick out your tail.

Champion

He finished his exercises and started to stand up; the Russian gymnast had just completed his series. The loudspeaker blared, "The next contestant is Steven Freeman of America doing . . ." He stood, like a pointer, perfectly motionless, in perfect concentration. Like a large cat stalking its prey he started his approach; he could see the crowd, on either side and to the front, a gigantic wave about to close in. He was close now, and the moment had come for his leap, off he went; he was an eagle pouncing on a rabbit. He hit and he could feel the comforting cold leather meet his hands. His body bent like a fishing pole and whipped around like a fishtailing car; the leather bit into his hands, but it was a solid feeling, something strong. Suddenly it was all done and he vaulted into the air, a falcon. This was the end, a perfect landing and he couldn't miss first place. He relaxed, but was still on guard. He hit and kept his balance, a cat on his four paws. He glanced at the crowd, then at his scores. First place! He slowly strode off, Hail Caesar, King of Rome.

(This is based on the picture of the blurred gymnast on pages 158–159.)

The following composition written on the "face" pictured on page 63 shows how one student saw a comparison and used it to develop his short essay. An entirely different approach is used in the short piece, "Silent Thoughts."

Masque

The eyes are the only parts of the face which seem to me to have any human resemblance. The eyelashes and shine of the pupils, and perhaps the shadow over the socket, create the effect of animation. The rest of the face, which has no expression in the sense that the features could change, is unhuman, partly because of the blaring light on the forehead bringing out the baldness, thus taking away something I associate with a face—hair around the head.

This picture reminds me of a picture I saw of a man in France after the last war, whose whole family had been wiped out by the enemy. He had no expression, the only sign of life being in his eyes. Otherwise, his face was an expressionless mask. The disaster had taken from that man all sentiments, and only his eyes remained to show life in his face. So, in a way, does the picture in the book remind me of men I know back home from the woods in Vermont, whose weather-beaten leathery countenances show no feeling, and only their eyes express the workings of their keen minds. In both these comparisons, the lack of sound is impressive. Bleak silence might express the feeling I get from the face in the annual.

Silent Thoughts

He doesn't know what it's like to sit here day after day. Silly, self-important people are always gawking at you; rubbing their fingers over your hair, and nose, and God-knows-what else; and then making those damn snotty cracks as if you were somehow responsible for your appearance. Don't they realize that you just get created? You don't have any say in the matter, do you, mister?

Read the following essay and then see whether you can answer the question at the end.

Dreadful Freedom

Freedom is exemption from action, release from pressure, reprieve from punishment. Freedom without determination or responsibility is meaningless. Viewed honestly and without pretense, true freedom is the collapse of all universal laws of responsibility. To be exact, freedom is itself nothingness, and is just as meaningless.

But, freedom with determination is very real. It involves the concept of choice: choice of the particulars of a man's existence—particulars which determine what a man is and what he does with his life. Thus, responsible freedom is not the gift of a deity or country. It is an individual's privilege of, and liability for, his actions.

According to the most basic doctrines of existentialism, a man's duty is *to* himself, his concern is *for* himself, he is guilty *of* himself, and he *is* his own necessity. Idealistically speaking, it is ignorant to say that a man is determined by his environment, for a man emphasizes, qualifies, restricts, or nullifies his environment by the values he reads into it. Just as slums have produced juvenile delinquents and criminals, equally detestable living conditions have produced great poets, brilliant composers, and financial geniuses.

This is why freedom is dreadful. It is the choice of bringing a purpose out of existence, or making a world out of nothing—through actions (for there is no transcendent "essence of humanity." The actions of men replace this).

The dread lies in the choices a man makes as to the course of his life, and in the awareness that a wrong choice, or no choice at all, can turn his world into nothingness, emptiness, and *self*-annihilation.

Now that you have seen all the pictures in this book, which one do you think stimulated this essay?

This book deliberately focuses on descriptive writing despite the fact that formidable opponents like Ernest Hemingway advise young writers to throw away their adjectives.

All good teachers know what Hemingway means, and this book does not aim at reviving the luscious prose of Samuel Taylor Coleridge. It does, however, aim at developing what might be called a descriptive eye, an eye for small, sharp, dramatic detail. Without such vision there will be very little good writing of any kind, either like Hemingway or Coleridge.

With it, young writers will at least be equipped to distinguish between good and bad description; but what is more important, they will have, in the professional's words, "something to say," and the teacher can fulfill his natural function of showing his students HOW to say it.

Too many textbooks and too many teachers have worked from the incomplete assumption that young writers, particularly in the ninth and tenth grades, should spend all their time perfecting their mechanics. As a result, hundreds of high-school graduates can produce competent expository prose that doesn't say anything worth reading. What is needed is a concentrated effort to show boys and girls how to find interesting subject matter. One way is to show them how to think; the other, which is the basis of this book, is to teach them how to see.

All good writing is based on a descriptive ability, from the Song of Solomon to Shakespeare to J. D. Salinger. It appears even in philosophical and scientific essays. Charles S. Peirce, for example, the American scientist and philosopher, gave his climactic definition of science in physically descriptive language:

> True science is distinctively the study of useless things. For the useful things will get studied without the aid of scientific men. To employ these rare minds on such work is like running a steam engine by burning diamonds.

Mr. Peirce's final phrase illustrates his ability to write abstractly and concretely at the same time, one of the greatest of all literary arts. The fuzziness, the vagueness of most student writing is due largely to the fact that boys and girls have never learned to observe physically and specifically. They charge heavily into monumental abstractions without any conception of how these intangible ideas relate to our tangible earth. On the contrary, no one, amateur or professional, can write intelligently until he has spent years understanding such relationships.

In a sense, students must pass through a descriptive phase before they can be cleared for other, more comprehensive writing. To emphasize this idea by an analogy, description is like physical technique to a musician: it is of limited value by itself, but no important ideas are any good without it.

The objective of this book is not, therefore, an end in itself; the goal is an expansive one—a way of seeing which will spread through an individual's entire life, from thinking to writing, to personal relationships, to studying, to emotional reactions, and to inspiration. As one professional photographer described it: "In the process of learning my work, I developed an entirely new way of looking at human experience."

It is not the sloppy, hurried way that most people look at pictures, AND life. It is the intense, concentrated way that distinguishes artists, philosophers, and superior men of business: the way of all terse, sensitive, and thoughtful men and women.

If students will learn to study pictures in the way advocated in this book, furthermore, no academician or pedagogue will be able to argue, as they so often do, that "pictures" have destroyed the art of thought, and have corrupted language; for nobody who has learned to translate accurate, imaginative visual images into precise, suggestive language can ever be charged as an enemy of verbal expressiveness.

Many teachers discuss visual education as if they hoped pictures were not here to stay. The greater part of wisdom, however, is to accept the inevitable and use it in the most intelligent, precise, and imaginative way possible. Throughout this book the controlling conviction is that the way is to show how vision, thought, and language are inseparably connected, and that when these connections are mastered, all three will be forever enriched.

To conclude with a final, practical word: harassed teachers who do not see how they can possibly handle a lot of writing in large classes, can find here a program of short, valuable exercises which can be used often without producing mountains of papers to correct. A single sentence every day from every student, written from concentrated observation, would be an intensely valuable experience in writing.

12 Leavitt / 13 Wanda McCoy, Scholastic / 14 Ted Grossbart, Scholastic / 17 Andrey Andersson, Black Star / 18 Phillips Academy / 19 Marc Riboud, Magnum / 20 Suzanne Szasz / 23 Genaro Olivares / 24 John Barsness, Scholastic / 25 Leavitt / 26 Robert Capa, Magnum / 27 Gregory Gilbert, Scholastic / 31 W. Eugene Smith / 32 Steve Lesser, Scholastic / 33 Philippe Halsman, Magnum / 34 Leavitt / 40 Deryk Wills / 41 Susan Greenburg Wood / 42 Carl Perutz / 43 David Linton / 44 Lou Bernstein / 45 Henri Cartier-Bresson, Magnum / 49 Buffalo Courier Express / 50 Rowena P. Brownell / 51 Bernard Hoffman, Life / 54 Weegee / 55 Leavitt / 56 Museum of Modern Art / 57 Robert Capa, Magnum / 63 Annemarie Heinrich / 64 W. Eugene Smith, Life / 65 Peter Barry, Scholastic / 72-3 Wide World / 74 Suzanne Szasz / 75 Ansel Adams / 76 Paul de Cordon / 77 Suzanne Szasz / 82-83 Yoichi R. Okamoto / 84 Leavitt / 85 Henri Cartier-Bresson, Magnum / 86, 87 Richard Graber / 92 Otto Hagel / 93 H. Foster Ensminger / 94 John Bryson / 95 Edward Steichen / 100 Hans Ahlborn / 101 Henri Cartier-Bresson, Magnum / 102 Sam Schulman, UPI / 103 Leavitt / 104 Eugene Cook / 105 Wide World Photos / 111 Louise Dahl-Wolfe / 112 Jules Alexander / 113 Leavitt / 114 William Vandivert / 115 Henri Cartier-Bresson, Magnum / 116 Inger Abrahamsen / 117 Toni Frissell / 118 Jeanloup Sieff / 119 Ollie Atkins, The Saturday Evening Post / 123 Henri Cartier-Bresson, Magnum / 124 Leavitt / 125 Cor Videler / 126-127 Joe Clark / 132 John Leongard; Charles R. Schulze / 133 Schulze; Allan Tuttle / 134-135 Charles R. Schulze / 136-139 Leavitt / 143 Edward Atler, Scholastic / 144 Robert Gorham / 145 Ted Croner / 146 Peter Stackpole, Life / 147 Clifton Foredy, Scholastic / 148 Leavitt / 152 William Vandivert / 153 Pete Daniels, Scholastic / 154 Richard Graber / 155 Dick Dallas, Scholastic / 156 Maria Austria / 157 Canon Photo Contest / 158-159 Flip Schulke / 163 Hans Wild, Life / 164, 165 Leavitt / 166 Peter Stackpole / 167 Nina Leen, Life / 171 Robert Häusser / 172 PSSC Physics, D.C. Heath / 173 W. Suschitzsky / 174 Helena Kolda / 175 David X Young / 176 Tony Peyron, Scholastic / 177 Jerry Aronson, Scholastic / 181 Sheldon Hine, APSA / 185 Hans Hubmann, Black Star / 187 International Silver Co. / 191 Michael Lichterman, Scholastic / 192 P.I.P. Photo / 193 David Linton / 194 Cor Videler / 195 W. C. Rauhauser / 199 Popular Photography / 200-201 Ruth Orkin / 202 Cor Videler